Awesome
Knights

KINGFISHER

First published 2016 by Kingfisher
an imprint of Macmillan Children's Books
20 New Wharf Road, London N1 9RR
Associated companies throughout the world
www.panmacmillan.com

Copyright © Macmillan Publishers International Ltd 2016

Interior design by Tall Tree Ltd
Cover design by Peter Clayman

Adapted from an original text by Philip Steele
Literacy consultants: Kerenza Ghosh, Stephanie Laird

Illustration by Steve Stone (represented by Artist Partners Ltd)
with addtional artwork by Thomas Bayley and Lee Gibbons

ISBN 978-0-7534-3965-4

Printed in China
9 8 7 6 5 4 3 2 1
1TR/1115/WKT/UG/128MA

A CIP catalogue record for this book is available from the British Library.

Picture credits
The Publisher would like to thank the following for permission to reproduce their material.
Top = t; Bottom = b; Centre = c; Left = l; Right = r
Front Cover Shutterstock/Grisha Bruev; Back cover Shutterstock/Ancher; 1c Heritage Image Partnership/Royal
Armouries; 4–5 Getty Images David Tomlinson; 5 With the Kind Permission of Warwick Castle; 6bl Bridgeman
Art Library, The Ashmolean Museum, Oxford; The British Museum; 7lb Heritage Image Partnership The
Royal Armouries; 7tr Heritage Image Partnership The Royal Armouries; 6–7b Corbis Barry Lewis; 14cl Alamy/
E. Katie Holm; 14cl Alamy/Jim Cole; 14r Alamy/David White; 14bl Alamy/Kari Niemelainen; 14bl Alamy/ Eric
Nathan; 15cl Alamy/Fabrice Bettex; 15b Alamy/Marina Spironetti; 15b Alamy/Eric Nathan; 16br With the Kind
Permission of Warwick Castle; 16cr Dorling Kindersley; 17t Corbis/Michel Setboun; 17b Heritage Image
Partnership The British Library; 18–19 Art Archive/University Library Prague/Alfredo Dagli Orti; 19tr Corbis/
The Gallery Collection; 20l Corbis/Darama/zefa; 20cl Heritage Image Partnership/The Print Collector;
20bl Heritage Image Partnership/Royal Armouries; 21tl Heritage Image Partnership/Royal Armouries;
21bl Heritage Image Partnership/Royal Armouries; 21br Heritage Image Partnership/Royal Armouries;
21background Corbis/Mimmo Jodice; 26cr Art Archive/Musée Condé Chantilly/Gianni Dagli Orti; 28l Corbis/
Dave Bartruff; 28c AKG, London, 28br AKG, London; 29l Art Archive/Musée Condé Chantilly/Gianni Dagli
Orti; 29tr Bridgeman Art Library/British Museum; 29surround Alamy/MEPL; 31br Heritage Image
Partnership/Royal Armouries.

CE
Common era, or Christian era.
The period of time since the
birth of Jesus Christ.

Contents

Middle Ages
The period from the fall of
the Roman Empire in 476CE
until about 1500.

A double-edged
longsword was
often used by a
knight to bring
down his enemy.

Knights
and castles

A knight was a noble armoured warrior who fought
on horseback during the Middle Ages. He served
his lord in battle and defended his lord's castle –
a stone fortified building that protected a town or
a region. Castles were used both as private homes
and as military bases for knights.

Loarre Castle in Aragon, an old kingdom in Spain, was built between about 1020 and the 1200s.

TOP FIVE BITESIZE FACTS

- The first castles were built from wood.
- A ditch surrounding a castle is called a moat.
- Windsor Castle, just outside London, is the oldest and largest inhabited castle in the world.
- There are about 1500 castle sites in Britain, of which only 300 are still standing.
- The largest castle in the world is Prague Castle, which is big enough to fit 13 football pitches.

Age of knights

Some knights became powerful and famous, as loyal friends or as fierce enemies, as champions of the king – or even as **traitors**.

Knights carried banners displaying their **coat of arms**. The coat of arms represented the knight's noble family name, so his opponent would know who he is.

First knights

The first knights were lightly armed and could attack quickly on horseback, as cavalry. But more heavily armoured warriors were also used to smash through enemy lines, and during the Middle Ages this type of attack became important in battle. These knights were armed with swords and protected by helmets.

crossguard

A firm footing

A stirrup holds a horseman steady in the saddle, making it easier for him to swing a sword in battle. The stirrup was invented in Asia and by the 700s it was being used throughout Europe. This single invention changed warfare forever.

This bronze stirrup was made in Asia more than 1300 years ago.

Rise of the knight

The age of the European knights began in the early 900s, when local lords and their mounted warriors defended people from raiders. Knights fought with swords, axes and long spears called **lances**. Some knights also carried clubs with spiky metal heads, called maces.

The ball at the end of the handle on this broadsword is called the pommel.

cavalry
Soldiers who attack on horseback. In the Middle Ages, cavalry was the fastest type of military force.

Mask of metal

In about 600CE, most fighting men wore simple helmets, but this **Anglo-Saxon** helmet was fit for a king. It is decorated with pictures of battles and it has eyebrows, a nose and a moustache. A crest runs over the top of the helmet and it has two dragon heads with red gemstones for eyes.

Replica of a ceremonial helmet from England in the early 600s.

The helmet is made from iron and its lining is made of leather.

iron with silver pattern

Elite weapons

This rare, decorated axe was made in the 600s. It was made by a tribe of people called the Franks who lived in what is now Germany. During the age of the knights, however, the sword was the most important weapon of a knight, and a symbol of his status.

The groove running down the middle of the blade is called the fuller, or 'blood gutter'.

TOP FIVE BITESIZE FACTS

A knight's **broadsword** could be up to 115 centimetres long, and was heavy.

A greatsword was even longer — it was so long that a knight needed both hands to use it.

The sword's pommel sometimes held a small badge showing the knight's coat of arms.

Knights would often carry a broadsword, a smaller sword for thrusting and a dagger.

The dagger could pierce gaps between armour.

The men of mail

The Normans were a warlike people from northern France who were descended from the **Vikings**. In the 1000s and 1100s they invaded southern Italy and England, where they built many castles.

chain-mail hood, or coif

helmet with a nose bar

Norman shields were kite-shaped and made of wood and leather.

Chain mail was strong but flexible.

Chain mail

The Norman knights wore a chain-mail coat called a hauberk. To make this, thick iron wire was shaped into rings. Each ring was linked with four others. The hauberk was worn over a padded tunic and leggings called chausses.

swords, around 1300s

mace, around 1100s

battleaxe, around 1000s

Weapons of war

In the 1000s, swords were mostly used for slashing and cutting. By the late 1200s, swords were being made to pierce through chain mail. A blow from a mace or from a **battleaxe** could also break through chain mail. Knights had to use shields as their main defence.

chain mail
Armour made from iron rings that are linked together.

An armoured glove was called a gauntlet.

The great helm covered the whole head and was padded on the inside.

The hauberk weighed about 10 kilograms – almost as much as four bricks.

The great helm
In the year 1250, European knights were still wearing chain-mail armour. Over the hauberk, they now wore a cloth tunic called a **surcoat**. Instead of the simple helmet with a nose bar, some knights now wore the great helm, which looked like a bucket with eye slits.

TOP FIVE BITESIZE FACTS

 The Normans, led by William, Duke of Normandy, invaded England in 1066.

The Normans defeated English forces led by King Harold at the Battle of Hastings.

The story of the invasion is shown in a **tapestry** called the Bayeux Tapestry.

The name 'Norman' comes from 'Norsemen', meaning 'men from the north'.

 Norman knights carried their horses to England in ships.

The Crusades

In 1095, Christian knights from western Europe travelled to fight the Muslims, or Saracens, living in the **Holy Land**. This region is now occupied by Syria, Israel, Lebanon, Palestine and Egypt. The wars that followed are called the Crusades, or 'wars of the cross'.

Saracens fought with a sword and round shield. They also used bows and arrows.

Crusader steel

Weapons included straight swords and falchions – a curved sword with one cutting edge. Knights also used flails – sticks with spiked balls. Some helmets of the 1200s were flat-topped. Others had rounded caps.

sword, early 1300s

falchion, 1200s

flail, 1500s

lance, around 1100s

helmet, around 1200s

Crusades
Military expeditions by medieval Christians to try and capture the Holy Land from the Muslims.

Held for ransom

As armoured knights battled in the heat and dust, cities were conquered and civilians were killed. If captured, a knight was sometimes held prisoner until a **ransom** was paid for his release.

Krak des Chevaliers in Syria was one of the strongest castles built by the Crusaders.

Crusader knights usually wore a cross on their tunic and shield to show they were Christians.

TOP FIVE BITESIZE FACTS

- Crusader knights even attacked other Christians. They ransacked the city of Constantinople (Istanbul) in 1204.

- The Crusaders left the Holy Land in 1291.

- There were nine major Crusades in total.

- Crusader knights formed religious groups, or orders, such as the **Knights Templar**.

- In 1212, thousands of children from France and Germany sailed to the Holy Land in the Children's Crusade — they were never seen again.

Homes of stone

By the 1100s stone castles had replaced early wooden structures and round towers had replaced square ones. The **keep**, or stronghold, was surrounded by huge walls and sometimes by a **moat** full of water, crossed by a drawbridge.

handsaw

carpenter's axe

awl

mason's axe

mallet

chisel

frame-saw

Wooden scaffolding helped the stonemasons to build the gatehouse.

This crane was powered by a worker walking inside a treadwheel.

Tools of the trade
Medieval craftsmen used basic metal tools and muscle power. Carpenters sawed and hammered, while masons chiselled the stone and checked that the walls were strong and straight.

Roof tiles were made from slate (shown here) or ceramic (baked clay).

Quarried stone was delivered by river barges and then on ox-carts.

Stones were held together using a cement made from sand, lime and water.

Castle walls could be 10 metres thick — about half the length of a bowling lane.

The tops of the walls were called **battlements**, from where defenders could shoot missiles.

A spiked metal barrier called a **portcullis** could be lowered by chains to protect the castle's thick main door.

The battlements had low **embrasures** and high **merlons**, so that archers could fire or take cover.

drawbridge
A bridge over a castle moat that could be raised to stop enemies entering the castle.

Castle life

steward
The person in charge of managing the castle.

A castle was not just a **fortress**, it was a home for many people. The castle of a lord would also be occupied by the lord's family, his squires (trainee knights) and his servants.

Lady of the house

While the lord was away at war, his home was run by his wife, the lady of the castle, or chatelaine. She held all the keys and ran the household from day to day.

Castle chapel

The castle had its own chapel, a tall chamber with stained-glass windows. The walls were decorated with stories from the Bible. In front of the altar, the priest led the prayers for the castle household and knights prayed here before battle.

Blacksmith

In a corner of the courtyard, a blacksmith hammered away at his **anvil**. He used it to make and repair iron tools, weapons, chains, wheel rims and horseshoes.

prison

store-room

chapel

14

KEY
- lower levels
- ground floor
- first floor

great hall

kitchen

courtyard

Round towers required spiral staircases made of stone. These were easy to defend.

solar

lord's bedroom

toilet

work-shop

Changing times

The first castles were built for defence and they were not very comfortable. By the 1400s, rich **nobles** wanted more luxurious homes, so some were turned into splendid buildings called palaces.

Lack of comfort

The castle rooms had little furniture. Linen, clothes and valuable goods were kept in big chests. The four-poster bed had curtains to keep out draughts.

Great hall

The centre of activity in many castles was the great hall. This was a lofty room with tall windows and a high, wooden roof. Its walls were hung with tapestries, and the floor covered with sweet-smelling rushes. Logs would burn in a huge fireplace, but the hall could be cold and draughty in winter.

TOP FIVE BITESIZE FACTS

- People in the Middle Ages ate off wooden plates or slabs of bread called trenchers.
- By the 1400s good table manners had become an important part of castle dining.
- One of the most precious items in the great hall was the salt cellar.
- The salt cellar was placed in front of the lord's most important guest at dinner.
- Musicians in the minstrels' gallery entertained the nobles, knights and other guests.

Heart of the castle

Today, the great hall of this English castle displays suits of armour and old weapons. In the Middle Ages, the halls were not just places to entertain with feasts and music. They also served as places for meetings between a lord and his knights to discuss battles. The great hall was also used to put criminals on trial.

From the kitchen

A noble banquet might include enormous pies, fine white rolls, roasted swan or wild boar. Meat was cooked in pots or roasted on spits. Ordinary people ate simple food, such as crusts of rough bread, cheese, broth or porridge.

roast pheasants and sauce

great hall of Warwick Castle, England

minstrels' gallery
A balcony overlooking the great hall, where the musicians played.

Great banquets

A **high table** for nobles, knights and royal guests stood at one end of the great hall, covered with fine linen. It was laid with silver cups, plates, spoons and knives. In the lower part of the hall, people sat on benches and ate off a wooden board.

This famous 'round table' has been hung on the wall of the great hall in Winchester Castle, England. It is painted with the names of the knights of the mythical King Arthur.

An English duke called John of Gaunt (1340–1399) is shown here feasting with the King of Portugal and four bishops.

Castle towns and lands

Many medieval castles were built on the site of **ancient strongholds**, where towns had already developed over the ages. In conquered lands, castles were built on new sites and new towns were built next to them.

Town charters

New towns were allowed by the king in a document called a charter, which was sealed with wax. This seal, from about 1316, is from Conwy, a walled castle town in northern Wales.

butcher chopping venison (deer meat)

edible snails for sale

A walled city

The city of Carcassonne in southwestern France has been a castle town since the days of the Celts and the Romans. Its large defences include double walls and 53 towers. The town was the scene of religious turmoil and warfare for hundreds of years.

fortify
To defend or make something strong against attackers.

Market day

Castle towns had busy streets with shops and market stalls selling food, woollen cloth or leather goods. There were blacksmiths, barrel-makers and wheelwrights, who made and repaired wheels. There were inns selling ale and wine, where travellers could rest and stable their horses.

Fruits of labour

The lands around the castle were governed by the lord of the castle, and **taxes** were paid to him. The lord also owned the watermills or windmills, which ground the wheat or barley. Farmers and labourers had to give food to the castle and the church.

fishmonger and barrel

TOP FIVE BITESIZE FACTS

- Castle towns were surrounded by high walls and strong gatehouses that joined to the castle defences.

- The lord of the castle earned money by taxing the people working in the town.

- During a war, knights often became rich by looting or pillaging towns.

- The medieval market at Norwich, England, had 130 different trades in the 1200s.

- Large markets, or fairs, would also have entertainers, such as musicians, acrobats, stilt walkers and fools.

The men of plate

Chain-mail armour could be pierced by a well-aimed arrow or a spear. After 1220, knights began to use a new type of armour. They protected parts of their body with plates of solid steel.

Metal workers

Here, an **armourer** hammers away in his workshop. Each city made armour with its own mark. Famous armourer towns included Milan in Italy, and Augsburg and Nuremberg in Germany. The most expensive plate armour was specially made to fit the wearer.

TOP FIVE BITESIZE FACTS

- The first plate armour covered only some parts of the body. By the 1400s, whole suits of armour were made covering everything.

- The steel plates were joined with leather straps, which allowed easier movement.

- A suit of armour was called a harness.

- Some suits could weigh 50 kilograms.

- A knight was armed by his squire, who dressed him from the feet upwards.

shirt of
chain mail

gauntlet

cuisse

poleyn

greave

solleret

Knights in shining armour

By the 1400s, plate armour gave the best protection for a knight. The finest suits of armour, or harnesses, were made for kings and princes, and they cost a fortune. However, even these could be pierced by a bolt fired from a crossbow or battered by blows from a sword.

pauldron

bevor

This knight is wearing armour dating from around 1475. His horse would have had its own plate armour.

Gauntlet

The first knights protected their hands with long chain-mail sleeves. From the 1300s, jointed plates were used to cover the hands, with metal cuffs over the wrists. This armour, called a gauntlet, was worn over a leather glove.

plate armour
Protective suit made of metal plates.

Battle!

Knights thundered into battle on huge warhorses. They aimed to knock the enemy knights from their saddles using lances, and then attack them with swords and maces. **Foot soldiers** tried to dismount knights with **pikes**.

Mud and blood

Battles soon became chaotic hand-to-hand fights. Victory was often decided by the weather – rain turned fields into mud causing armour to sink. This scene recreates the Battle of Poitiers, fought between England and France in the Hundred Years' War.

TOP FIVE BITESIZE FACTS

 Defending troops would put up wooden stakes called palings to stop enemy cavalry.

 Archers used longbows to create a hail of arrows to pierce a knight's plate armour.

 A longbow could fire an arrow more than 300 metres.

 The Hundred Years' War actually lasted from 1337 to 1453.

The Battle of Poitiers ended with an English victory and the capture of the French king.

Spikes called caltrops were laid on the battlefield to injure the enemy's horses.

caltrop with four spikes

longbow
A large, light bow that could shoot an arrow over long distances.

23

Sieges

To win control of a region, an army had to capture its castles. Knights and other soldiers surrounded the walls and cut off all supplies and support. The aim was to force the enemy to surrender.

All-out assault

These attackers have stripped the countryside bare of food. They now launch a final attack with huge catapults, battering rams and siege towers. Arrows rain down on the castle.

mangonel

trebuchet

Various types of catapult were used to throw missiles at the walls or over the battlements. Cannons did not come into use until the 1340s.

TOP FIVE BITESIZE FACTS

 Attackers would dig tunnels under walls in order to make the walls collapse.

Siege towers were nicknamed belfries, because they looked like the bell tower of a church.

A mangonel was a type of catapult that hurled rocks from a cup at the end of its arm.

A trebuchet used a big weight to hurl rocks.

Attacking soldiers stood behind a protective wall called a pavise.

siege tower

scaling ladder

siege
The attack of a castle or city by surrounding it, often cutting it off from supplies of food and water.

Gatehouse defence

Portcullises were grids of timber and iron that were lowered to trap enemy troops inside the gatehouse. There, they would meet a hail of arrows, crossbow bolts or spears. Rocks, boiling water or even heated sand could be dropped onto the attackers through openings known as meurtrièrs, or murder holes.

25

Tournaments

Knights needed to practise their fighting skills. Mock battles, or *mêlées*, were held as well as bouts of single combat, known as jousting. Large fighting festivals, called tournaments, became very popular.

For the ladies

A knight might dedicate his jousting contest to a lady of the court seated in the stands. He would have been identified by his coat of arms.

jousting
A competition between two knights on horseback who were usually armed with lances.

At full tilt

In the 1400s, a type of jousting called tilting became fashionable. Knights on horses, separated by a fence, raced towards each other, aiming to dismount their opponent. Lances had blunt tips, but injuries could still be bad, so padded helmets and strong armour were worn.

TOP FIVE BITESIZE FACTS

A jousting lance could be four metres long.

During a joust, the lance was held in the couched position — close to the knight's body and tucked underneath the arm.

The disc found in front of the hand on a lance was called the vamplate.

In 1559, French king Henry II was killed by accident during a joust.

Other weapons used in a joust included swords, daggers and maces.

The code of honour

From the 1100s onwards, knights across Europe were expected to behave honourably and to follow Christian teachings. They were supposed to be courteous, gentle and noble, and to protect the weak from the strong.

The Black Prince

Edward the Black Prince (1330–1376) was named after the colour of his armour. The son of the English king, he was famous for his chivalry in battle, treating enemy knights with respect.

tomb statue of the Black Prince

Page to squire

At about seven years old, a boy was sent to a castle to serve as a page. He would learn good manners and fighting skills. When he was about 14, he could become a squire, helping a knight on and off the battlefield. Once he had proved himself in battle, he could become a knight.

A French knight of the 1300s is armed by his squire.

'Dubbing' a knight

When a king made a man into a knight he tapped a sword on each of the man's shoulders – an act called dubbing. This signified his knighthood.

In love with love

Knights were in love with the idea of love. Poets were always writing about knights who honoured a pure, noble lady with little hope of winning her affection. This 'fine' or 'courtly' love had little to do with real, passionate love.

Love — or death!

This shield was made in the 1400s. It shows a young knight declaring his love for his lady. He swears that if she rejects his love, the figure of Death (behind the knight) will carry him away.

A noble lady is seated in her castle.

A knight kneels before her, pledging his service.

chivalry

The ideal virtues of the knight, such as courage, honour, respect, generosity and courtesy.

TOP FIVE BITESIZE FACTS

 A dubbing ceremony would be held after the knight had spent a night praying in a chapel.

The knights' code was called chivalry.

A chivalrous knight always spoke the truth and protected the weak and defenceless.

He also never turned his back on an enemy.

 The age of chivalry ended by the 1500s when knights had been replaced by infantrymen and cannons.

Glossary

ancient stronghold
A historical place that has been fortified against attack. Castles often stand on the sites of more ancient forts.

Anglo-Saxon
Germanic peoples who invaded England from the 400s.

anvil
A heavy iron block on which hot metal is hammered into shape by a blacksmith.

armourer
In the Middle Ages, a person skilled in forging weapons and plate armour from iron and steel.

battleaxe
A large, broad-bladed axe used in battles of the Middle Ages.

battlements
The upper part of a fortified wall.

broadsword
A long sword with a wide blade.

coat of arms
An image representing a knight's family name, often shown on a shield.

embrasure
A low section of a castle's battlements through which an archer can shoot.

foot soldiers
Soldiers who do not fight on horseback. They are supported by archers.

fortress
A defensive building designed as a military base rather than a private home.

high table
In a castle, the lord's table, which is on a platform at the end of the great hall.

Holy Land
Those lands of western Asia held to be sacred by Jews, Christians and Muslims.

keep
A castle's central tower, with thick walls.

Knights Templar
A specially chosen group of warrior-monks who became powerful during the Crusades.

lance
A type of long spear, used by knights when charging on horseback.

medieval
Dating from the Middle Ages.

merlon
A high section of a castle's battlements that provides cover for an archer.

moat
A water-filled trench surrounding a castle.

noble
A person of the highest social class.

pike
A long spear used by foot soldiers against cavalry in the 1400s.

portcullis
A heavy grid of timber and iron.

quarried
Cut from a quarry of rocks. Quarried stone was transported to the site of a castle, where it was used to build walls.

ransom
Money demanded for the release of a prisoner.

spiral staircase
A winding staircase inside a castle tower.

surcoat
A cloth tunic worn over armour. During the Crusades, a surcoat stopped metal armour from overheating in the sun.

tapestry
A hand-woven textile featuring patterns or pictures, used as wall hangings in many old castles.

taxes
Money or goods that must be paid to those governing the land.

traitor
Someone who breaks an agreement, betraying his or her loyalty.

Vikings
Medieval warriors from Denmark, Sweden or Norway. The Normans were descendants of the Vikings who lived in northern France.

Index